THE QUIET

Memories of A South Down Farm
in the 1860s

M AUDE Robinson was born in 1859 on the family farm in Saddlescombe, Sussex, and she continued to live there for much of her life. In the early years of this century she was a widely admired writer on the rural life and natural world of Sussex. A life-long Quaker, she wrote three books of Quaker stories, *The Time of Her Life, Wedded in Prison and other Quaker Stories* and *Nicholas, the Weaver*. *The Quiet Valley*, one of her best known books, was originally published in 1938 under the title *A South Down Farm in the Sixties*. She died in 1950.

Books by Maude Robinson
   The Time of Her Life
   Wedded in Prison and other Quaker Stories
   Nicholas, the Weaver

SADDLESCOMBE IN THE 1930s

THE QUIET VALLEY

Memories of a South Down Farm
in the 1860s

by
MAUDE ROBINSON

TURNASTONE PRESS

First published in 1938
by J.M.Dent & Sons Ltd,
under the title *A South Down Farm in the Sixties*.

Second Impression in 1947
for the Bannisdale Press
by kind permission of J.M.Dent & Sons Ltd.

This edition published in 1994 by
Turnastone Press
77, Sirdar Road
London W11 4EQ

British Library Cataloguing-in-Publication Data
A catalogue record for this book is available from the
British Library.
ISBN 0 9523638 0 1

Cover design by Andrew King

Printed and bound in Great Britain by
Antony Rowe Ltd, Wiltshire

CONTENTS

ACKNOWLEDGEMENT

I am indebted to many people for their support during the production of the new edition of Maude Robinson's childhood memoirs. I am particularly grateful to my daughter Gabrielle, my nephew Andrew, and to Peter, my husband. All of whom have contributed so much to bringing the book back into print.

Judy Seymour, 1994
TURNASTONE PRESS

ILLUSTRATIONS

PREFACE

FEW memories go back to the days when farming was a simple matter — subject only to a few regulations from an understanding landlord, or none, if the farmer were a yeoman cultivating his own land. In either case he went his way untrammelled by rules and regulations. Many a man who could barely write his name, but was deeply learned in country lore, then farmed successfully, but now he needs the training of an accountant, and such legal and scientific knowledge as was unknown in the sixties.

It seems rather absurd that home-grown corn cannot now be fed to the poultry, but must be sold and bought back again if the advantage of the wheat quota is to be claimed. As for the restrictions on the selling of milk, it is impossible to refer to these correctly if you are not in the trade!

Times have changed. The war put a stop to the homely simplicity of English country life, although farmers should and do appreciate some of the restrictions, such as those to prevent the spread of cattle disease — trying as they are at the time.

With these and other recent changes it seemed to me worth while to jot down memories of country life as it was in my childhood. These first appeared in somewhat different form in that excellent local periodical 'The Sussex Magazine', which happened to be seen by the Hon. Editor of 'The Friends' Quarterly Examiner' — that unique Review which was started in 1867 with the avowed intention of never paying its contributors! Failure was freely foretold, but still it pursues its calm way, the pages as well filled as ever! For many years I have contributed articles to this periodical and I was asked to 'Quakerize' the South Down narrative, dwelling on the items in our life which would interest specially members of our own denomination. So much interest was expressed by readers that I have been induced to entirely re-write the memories in the hope that in book form these may please a new circle of readers who have not seen the other versions.

Maude Robinson

11 Windlesham Gardens
Brighton I

INTRODUCTION

IN Maude Robinson's 'Quiet Valley' in the South Downs the once quiet country road is frequently jammed with cars and lorries taking a short cut from the Weald into Brighton. Down the farm track, now part of the South Downs Way, many hundreds, possibly even thousands of walkers, riders and cyclists journey every year. Yet probably only a handful of them is aware of much more than a picturesque cluster in the folds of the hills, a breathing place before the next steep climb. To read this book is to see Saddlescombe Farm very differently.

The author published it first in 1938, at a time when the Sussex countryside faced increasing pressures from visitors and developers. That the spot she described has survived at all is because Brighton Corporation purchased the land in the 1920s, as part of a green ring that still contains the urban sprawl. By then the farming life she described had virtually disappeared. Agricultural depression, rural depopulation, the First World War and new technology had all combined to break with the past. The book fed a nostalgia for that lost 'real

England' which is still growing. It is not as well known as its near-contemporary, Flora Thompson's *Lark Rise*, but it offers an interesting counterpoint to that famous study of an Oxfordshire hamlet.

The story of Maude Robinson's childhood is simply and well told — there is little literary artifice about it. Her Quaker honesty captures evocatively the daily rhythms and practices that governed the life of the farm, but the historian may wish to explore the broader social context at a time when rural poverty was widespread.

In the pages we meet a hardworking, principled and, at times, autocratic farmer, Maude's father Martin. He paid his labourers the going local rate, which kept them amongst the poorest of Victorian workers, and he was strict. There was none of the customary beer for the workers nor any of the raucous feasting common elsewhere when the harvest finished. But there were some generous payments. His daughter remembers no poverty, except from drink and improvidence, and that would have made the place unusual. Yet at a time of increasing migration to the developing towns of the South Coast, the reader might wonder how stable a community it was. Apart from the comparatively prosperous foreman, Henry Pelling, and eccentric shepherds we get little sense as to how long individuals stayed there. Were the lights and job possibilities of nearby Brighton as alluring as they proved elsewhere in the county?

Martin Robinson seems at least to have provided his workers with decent housing at prices they could afford and we do get hints of the additions to income which were often as important as money wages. The corn, for example, gleaned by women and children 'who toiled all day' at harvest time, was still an essential part of subsistence in this pre-mechanised world.

The other main interest of the book lies in its portrayal of a young girl's growing up in circumstances that were comfortable by the standards of those who lived a few yards away and who were far more removed socially. Maude had opportunities for education and leisure which they did not. She shared the firm values of many religiously-minded, hard-working members of the Victorian rural middle classes. There is a sharpness of vision as well as some sadness in the eye of this woman's remembering events seventy years before. But the judgements are always gentle and there is much happiness and comedy in her writing. What we are offered is clarity in her portrayal of a world she knew had long gone as she wrote. As a child she could not have known that it was disappearing even as she grew up.

Maude Robinson lived at Saddlescombe for 67 years, only leaving after her brother died in 1925. She became a prolific writer of minor pieces, with an eye for the natural world which suffuses this book. To treat it only as a pleasant, nostalgic piece would be wrong. It offers us some valuable insights into rural history but it should still serve the purpose which led to its first publication. It reminds us of values that sometimes seem alien and it reminds us how we have lost much of the good as well as the bad of the past. It also offers continued inspiration for efforts to save the still-threatened beauty and life of the Downs.

John Lowerson, 1994
University of Sussex

I. AT SADDLESCOMBE

IT is only a remote sheep farm — a little dimple in the Downs six miles from Brighton. It is bounded on the north by beautiful, wooded Newtimber Hill, lately made over to the National Trust as a playground for ever in memory of good Earl Buxton. To the north west there is a rare view of what Rudyard Kipling calls 'the blue goodness of the Weald', showing in the far distance Leith Hill, Hindhead, and the Hog's-back in Surrey, with Chanctonbury Ring on the nearer range of hills. On all the other sides are softly rolling Downs, with not a rock, hedge, or tree to break their outlines. To the native they have a particular charm. I remember when at the age of seventeen I first saw rocky hills they gave me the impression of a starved animal, with its bones protruding through its skin!

The hamlet of Saddlescombe has a long history. In the pages of the Domesday Book it was 'Selscombe'. There was land for ten ploughs, thirteen acres of meadow (about the present amount), and wood for five hogs. 'In the time of King Edward it was worth £15. Now £11.'

The open Downs were taken for agriculture when

the Weald below was one vast forest with which the tools of those primitive days could not cope, until much later the fine oaks were ruthlessly sacrificed to melt the iron ore beneath them.

About the year 1225 a local magnate piously made a grant of the Manor to the powerful Soldier Monks, the Knights Templars, but in the reign of Edward II their reputation was so bad that the Pope dissolved the Order and Saddlescombe was handed over to the slightly more respectable Knights of St. John. The inventory of the Templars' possessions is most interesting. They culti-vated 163 acres of arable land, and had a windmill worth 13s 4d — a very early instance of the utilization of wind power. They had two barns, an oxshed, a stable, a garden, and a 'pipe of cider worth 4 shillings'. They had only one horse, but kept twelve oxen for plough-ing — just as my father did many centuries later. They had 600 sheep, and to enclose them '40 hurdles and 6 wattles', the very same fencing which is used there to this day.

The Templars' household possessions were of the simplest — 'three trestle tables, one chair, two brass pots, two dishes, one towel, and one cup'. No bedding is mentioned. The fittings of the chapel were 'a cup worth ten shillings and a missal worth twenty shillings'.

Archaeologists have searched in vain for any trace of this chapel, or other medieval buildings. The native flint and chalk does not stand the weather of ages like hewn stone, and the only relic of the monkish owners was believed to be the well. The 150 feet dug down through solid chalk was a work that would hardly have been undertaken for a mere hill farm. Although now superseded by an hydraulic ram, which automatically brings pure water from the springs below, the well house is still there, with its huge oaken wheel. 'How like Carisbrook', is the frequent comment of visitors.

When the religious communities were banished, Saddlescombe was bought by Sir Anthony Brown, the owner of the Castle in the adjoining parish of Poynings. It is probable that he built the picturesque east end of the farm house, for the enormous oaken beams and stone-built fireplaces point to the Tudor period.

To this remote valley in the year 1853 my father, Martin Robinson, a Surrey farmer, came. He had been cultivating the flat fields of his native place, and thought he saw in the primeval turf a field for enterprise, for it was in the palmy days of corn-growing and wheat was the farmer's chief idea. Ours was also a sheep farm — 'A sheep to an acre' was the old rule — and on the 900 acres were kept three flocks of 300 sheep each. They

3

were folded on the arable land by night, but all the day long each flock was followed by a shepherd with his shaggy dog and polished crook. In the sixties the shepherds were a race apart. One of ours was named Thomas Shepherd, and another Fred Wooler, as if their ancestors had followed the calling since surnames were invented. So absorbed were they in the welfare of their flocks that when we started sending milk to Brighton the shepherds regarded every crop grown for the cows as infringing the rights of their sheep!

When my father took the farm there were only six cottages, and these he reduced to five, as he would never be responsible for a dwelling with less than three bedrooms, but in after years, the milk trade needing more labour, seven more cottages were built. The older ones were rented at 1 s a week — I think the newer ones were 1 s 6d, and every man had as much garden as he could cultivate and was encouraged to plant fruit trees. With this, although wages were what would now be considered scandalously low, from 1 os to 18s a week according to skill, the labourers were very comfortably off and I remember no real poverty. They could have gorse for fuel, and I remember one man saying with great satisfaction when winter set in, 'Yes, I've six boys, but I've got a sack o' taters put by for each of them'.

SADDLESCOMBE FROM THE SOUTH-WEST

SHOEING AN OX AT SADDLESCOMBE

All was hand labour on farms then, and very skilled were some of these men in their own departments. 'Old Daddy' who worked in the garden, and mowed the lawn with a scythe, patiently warning our little feet, 'Get out o' my way, my dear', was a perfect picture of Father Christmas, snowy hair and beard and bright red cheeks. He always wore a grey linen smock and a rather shapeless hat, plaited with his own fingers from local wheat straw and stitched together by his wife. In the winter the estate carpenter gave these hats a coat of lead-coloured paint, to make them waterproof. Old Daddy's son, Henry Pelling, was 'foreman for fifty years on Saddlescombe farm', as is recorded on his tombstone in Newtimber churchyard. One of his sons was oxman. In the sixties the bullocks used were of the red Sussex breed, but later it was found that the large, black, long-horned Pembrokes, which had been brought in large droves from North Wales to Sussex fairs, were stronger and hardier. The pairs were chosen as nearly of a size as possible that the heavy wooden yokes might be level, and their names were always one with a single syllable and one with two: 'Hawk and Pheasant', 'Quick and Nimble', 'Crisp and Curly', 'Peart and Lively', and if one name was called the two responded. I have heard Charles Pelling, when the whole team were lying in the thick straw in the yard, call, as he took down the yoke, 'Peart!' and up would jump Peart, and also Lively with him, standing side by side to be harnessed. Each pair was supposed to have the strength of one good horse, but they lived on rougher food, and were beef when done with, and good beef too, after some months in the fatting stall. They were slow, but pulled with steady strength — no jerks, so that when the traction engine of later days got into a ditch, it was the ox team that was sent to pull it out. Our teams were seldom sent on the roads, but I have seen six great red oxen pulling a waggon of exceedingly dirty ice to the ice pit at the top of North Street — now one of the most crowded streets in great Brighton.

The bovine intellect cannot be taught to lift one foot at a time to the blacksmith's knee, which is an early lesson for all horses. When a bullock was to be shod, it was thrown down on soft grass, the smallest ox-boy rushed in and sat on it's massive neck to keep it from struggling, the four feet were bound to a tripod of poles, and the blacksmith nailed on the shoes at his leisure. Of course there were two 'cues' as they were called to each foot, of rather thin iron, somewhat the shape of a comma. We always knew that bullock shoeing was in prospect when the blacksmith, Miles Mobsby, sent to ask for a piece of fat pork for a pincushion. In the farm house cellar the thick sides of pork were in a huge tub, kept under the pickle with a flat stone. The long sharp nails were stuck in a piece of this pork so that each was slightly greased. The great creature took this drastic treatment very calmly. When ropes were untied, and the boy rolled off the neck, it rose slowly, gave a mighty shake, and at once began to graze. It was the blessed invention of the self-binding reaper which ended the picturesque custom of using bullock teams. Six or eight great animals were too clumsy to turn at the corners, especially on the last turns in the middle of the field, so long before the war they vanished, except one team which was kept on for its picturesqueness by a gentleman farmer near Eastbourne. Our old ox-man wept when the last team was sent away to the butcher, and he had to turn to horses and other farm work, but he was adaptable and worked on for many years.

These men, born to the place, were very shrewd as to the best methods, and a wise master often followed their advice. Each had his speciality. Some in the winter could wield the flail with which oats and barley were beaten out on the polished oaken floor of the barn, although in the sixties a threshing machine was in use for wheat, turned by three horses plodding

b

round a large circle outside the barn door. In the seventies a steam engine, drawn by horses, was hired, and the wheat was much more rapidly obtained. To those used to the flail it seemed like a miracle to see the bright, clean, well sifted corn running down a pipe into the sacks hung on below. The mowing of the hay was done by four men following each other with well sharpened scythes. Very hard work it was, but one little, wiry old man, Jack Sayers, who always worked in a battered top hat, managed to keep pace with the rest. Jack, with his low wages, after his family grew up, saved enough to hire a few acres, buy a horse and van, and send vegetables to Brighton. So industrious a man might have prospered, but, alas, Jack the second had a weakness; the public houses on the road were too strong a temptation and little of the money taken reached home. Father and son both ended their days at the expense of the public in the Workhouse, which the father certainly did not deserve. Another good workman did the same. Jimmy was a bachelor, and a most kindly soul, beloved of all the children, for whom he used to make little wooden clogs to wear in muddy weather. He also had a knack of lighting his pipe by striking his knife with a flint picked up in the field, using a tuft of very dry thistle-down as tinder — a relic of the old days when the tinder box was a necessity in every household, although in farm houses the great heaps of wood ashes on the kitchen hearth did not go out from one year's end to another. But, old Jimmy also had a weakness, and had his earnings not been wasted at the public house in the neighbouring parish, he might have had a comfortable provision for his old age. Even in the Workhouse Jimmy was a favourite from his cheerful, obliging ways.

Another mower, Webb Souch, was also an expert in the art of killing and dressing pigs, when each labourer's ambition was to raise his own pork and bacon, and it was hung to be smoked in the master's smoke house. The butcher lived five miles away and a good store of bacon and smoked sausages was necessary in every farm house. Neither Webb nor his wife, whose name was Philadelphia, could read, but they made their very dull son walk four miles to a school where there was a master, fancying the local school-ma'am had not capacity to make him learn. Never was there a cleaner cottage. Philadelphia scrubbed the brick floor daily, and every day her men folk had clean cotton stockings. The son, who later worked on the farm, had charge of a gaunt old yellow horse, reputed to have been an artillery horse which had survived the Crimea. The lad, as he groomed her, remarked, 'Poor old Dimond, she was in the wars. 'Spect she has often been hit by a cannon ball!'

Sheepshearing day was one of the events of the year. If the weather was doubtful the flocks would be sheltered in the large barns the previous night. I have seen a most curious effect when the many hundreds of pairs of luminous yellow eyes turned towards us in the darkness, the bodies of the sheep being quite invisible.

A gang of about twenty capable men was collected to go from farm to farm in the month of June. The leader was 'Captain' — a title he retained for life, and strangers were puzzled when 'old Capt Hollingdale' was found never to have set foot on a vessel in his life. He wore a broad gold lace band round his tall hat, and his 'Lieutenant' a silver one! How strange it seems to us in these practical days that these men worked in the hot sun in battered top hats, and even played cricket in the same! The Captain needed to be a man of ability to collect men and money and satisfy the discontent of the beer-fuddled brains of his crew. For in the old days shearing was never accomplished without much beer. This my father steadily refused to provide, and although he offered handsome money payment instead the local gang refused to come, but were glad to return when another gang stepped in for one season. Then one of

A BULLOCK TEAM AT SADDLESCOMBE

SHEEP-SHEARING AT SADDLESCOMBE
The picture shows 'stokos' —oatmeal and lemon drink

the best shearers broke his leg when drunk, saw the folly of it, and never touched beer again. Gradually the rest realized his advantage and were glad to share the 'Stokos', oatmeal and water flavoured with lemon, brought fresh and cool from the dairy in fine old brown Sussex ware pitchers. One man from a distance observed, 'Shouldn't mind if that 'ooman allers made my drink!'

The grindstone was busy on the morning of shearing day, for to keep shears keen and sharp was very important. Most men brought two pairs and had a broad strap on the right wrist to prevent strain. The head shepherd saw that every man was provided with a sheep, and the musical 'clip, clip' of the twenty pairs of shears began, broken only by an occasional call of 'Tar boy!' promptly answered by 'Coming, sir!' from the lad, who would rush in and drop a pinch of lime where a sudden struggle of the sheep had caused a small wound. This was to keep away the dreaded fly from the sore, a great enemy of sheep, as all know who have seen its horrible ravages. A shearer was considered a bad workman and was chaffed if he called 'Tar boy', too often. I believe a skilled hand could shear forty or fifty sheep in the day, neatly and carefully clipped, for the rough work of Australian shearers would not have satisfied the flock-

masters in the palmy days of South Down sheep farming. The shepherd's wife, who was also a shepherd's
daughter, stood ready to pick up each fleece, throwing
in stray locks, and to carry it to a clean patch of grass,
where it was spread out like a blanket and an elderly
man would roll it into a compact bundle, binding it
with a skilfully twisted rope of its own material, and
adding it to the great pile to be later stored in the
granary until the day when the wool merchants would
pack it for Bradford.

The price of wool has varied immensely within the
memory of the writer. When the American Civil War
caused the cotton famine it fetched 2s per pound, then
it sank to about 9d and sheep farming did not pay, for
shepherds' wages had risen and sheep ate as much as
before. Now the price has risen again, to the relief of the
flock-master.

Although not so soft as Merino, Southdown wool is of
good quality and is used for knitting wools and the best
blankets. Of course the best fleeces come from the 'tegs'
— young sheep who had never been shorn before. Having
had three months more to grow, the staple was longer
and the tegs had not had the wear and tear of rearing
lambs. The large high-bred rams yielded fine fleeces, as
much as 10 or 12 lb of wool being sheared from one

of them. When the last lock was clipped and the shearer stood up it was amusing to see the antelope-like bounds with which the sheep, released from the heavy coat which must have been an oppressive burden on summer days, dashed away to join its fellows. As in Bible days, the sheep is still 'dumb before its shearers', but when reassembled a chorus of 'baas' in every key follows, as though the sheep are telling each other of the amazing experience they have come through. Farmers dread cold nights after the warm fleece is removed, and sheep have been known to have been trampled to death as they crowded together for warmth.

II. HARVEST TIME AND
THE WELL-WHEEL

FOR the eight children who grew up in the quiet valley of Saddlescombe life was never dull, as something of interest was always to be found in wild nature and in the varied activities of the farm at different seasons of the year. Harvest lasted long in the premachine days when all the corn was cut by hand with a 'swop hook', which to the initiated is quite a different thing from a sickle, and it was a busy time for the farmer and his elder sons when every man's work had to be measured off with a chain.

However ample the supply of labour for the rest of the year it was impossible for the ordinary staff to manage the harvest, and crowds of Irish labourers came to England at this season, sleeping in the out-buildings as the hop-pickers do. I have seen a dozen camp fires in one small paddock for their primitive cooking — tea made in a black can, and the lid of the same turned upside down in the embers to fry rashers of bacon. It was an anxious time for the farmer, for the Irish would have candles beside their straw beds, and although our parish of Newtimber was a Prohibition area they came back from their shopping in the next village none too sober. My father used to make the round of the buildings last thing at night to be sure that every light was out. The self-binding reaper has changed all this, and is a blessed invention, clearing the cornfields efficiently. The country folks say that it leaves so little scattered corn that gleaning, or 'leasing' as it is called in Sussex, is not worth doing, but the cheaper price of bread and the higher wage make this work less necessary.

In the old days we children spent much time in the harvest field picking up the scattered corn and giving our bunches in turn to the women and children who toiled all day. I have known an industrious woman with well trained children pick up in one harvest season eleven bushels of wheat! Her husband would beat it out with a flail on the master's threshing floor and it would be sent in grists to the windmill three miles away. Roughly it would provide nearly eleven bushels of flour, and what an immense relief it was to the thrifty mother to have no bread bill for which to contrive payment for many weeks! Of course she baked at home, each cottage being provided with a brick oven. That was the time when boots and overcoats and much needed bedding could be bought. Mattresses they had none, but ticks well filled with soft oat chaff were in regular use, clean and wholesome, but smelling a little of the barn.

It was never my father's custom to give harvest suppers. They were too apt to end in drunkenness and the wives and children had no share, so at the close of harvest two large sheep were killed and a liberal joint of mutton, enough for many meals, was given to each family.

Undoubtedly the spot of greatest interest in the valley was the well-house, a square building open on one side with a huge broad wheel in which donkey, pony or man stepped on and on like a squirrel in a cage, bringing up from 150 feet below the pure water on which eleven households depended for drinking purposes, although large tanks gave ample supplies of soft rain water. Over the massive oaken beam which formed the axle of the wheel was a single chain and at each end a large oaken, iron-bound bucket, holding about twelve gallons, the empty one going down when the full one came up. I never remember seeing my sweet-tempered father so angry as when he found that one of the farm lads, from sheer bravado, had gone down in the empty bucket on the single, well worn chain, without any precaution of testing the air by a lighted candle. That lad died lately, an elderly man, but he certainly never forgot those pungent words on the sin of foolhardiness, and he also probably remembered it when a well-digger in a neighbouring village fell a victim to neglect of the candle test and perished in spite of the effort of a 'Carnegie Hero' to rescue him.

In 1853 the water was drawn daily by an old white donkey, named Smoker, doubtless after that Brighton bathing man who used physical force to restrain the Prince Regent when he attempted to bathe in a dangerous sea. This donkey was prehistoric! Nobody knew his age, he simply always had been there! There is an old saying that few have seen a dead donkey, but that experience was mine 70 years ago when we children watched the workmen bury the gaunt white corpse of Smoker. We were not mourners, for he was a bad-tempered old beast and the workmen had often warned us to keep away from his heels and his teeth. He did no other work and had an uncanny faculty for opening gates and doors in order to revel in green garden vegetables, so each garden gate had a sliding bar to keep him out.

More than half a century later, when one of the children was a London M.D. his chauffeur told him that a very old man who lived near him claimed to be a native of Saddlescombe. Thinking he probably meant the much more populous place of Sedlescombe, near Hastings, my brother said, 'Ask him what the old donkey's name was'. Next morning came the reply, 'He says the donkey's name was Smoker, Sir'.

The well-wheel could be turned by a man but it was tedious work and Smoker was replaced by a large grey donkey whom my father named 'Issachar' because, like the son of Jacob, he was 'a strong ass'. He had been broken to harness and was fairly amenable and there was a little cart in which we children collected material for our fifth of November bonfire. We toiled for weeks beforehand, fetching dry weeds, hedgeclippings and stray bits of gorse from all over the farm, for our thrifty father would not tolerate the waste of fuel which might be put to a better use. But if the weather was moderately dry it made a fine blaze and it was supplemented with a few cheap squibs, crackers, and Catherine wheels. So we had a glorious time, the farm lads joining in shouting the traditional rhyme, 'Remember, remember the fifth of November', although probably they had not the faintest knowledge of the story of Guy Fawkes. We three youngest used to ride Issachar all at once, Ernest, the born farmer, in front to guide the steed, Louis, the future M.D., balanced over the donkey's tail, while I was wedged between, seated sideways, for my father had a great idea of maidenly propriety, and at the mature age of six or seven it was decreed that I was to ride

'COM,' AGED 35, WITH ADAMS

THE AUTHOR IN THE 1860s

astride no more. This, when I rode alone, necessitated that conventionality a saddle, for which my brothers had no use, much preferring to ride bareback. But a donkey can never be quite depended on — Issachar was wilful and hard mouthed, and would suddenly decide, when carrying one of my sisters in a riding party with horses, that a roll would be agreeable, and it was a struggle for the little rider to keep him from carrying out his design and breaking the saddle.

So the older children begged for a pony, small enough to tread the well-wheel but so much pleasanter to ride.

My father went to Reigate fair and among a drove of unbroken Welsh colts one took his fancy. The poor, unshod young things had tramped all the way from Wales, from fair to fair, but that had not broken the spirit of the colt of his choice, who was rearing and walking around on his hind legs — a pretty little beast, dark brown with a white star on his forehead. The owner asked £5 but it was reduced to 95s and seldom has that modest sum been better spent. The money was paid. 'Now pull him over backwards', said my father to the lad who held the halter. It was done. There was little danger of injury on the soft turf of Reigate Heath and the astonished pony was soon up again, but the lesson was learnt, and it was years before he took to rearing again, a dangerous trick in a child's pony, though it must be confessed that when middle-aged as horses go, he did rear in moments of great excitement. He was named 'Commodore Nut', after a little dwarf who was then being exhibited with the more celebrated Tom Thumb, and as 'Com' he was known to a large circle. For thirty-two years he was the family pet and friend. When at the age of 35 his teeth gave out and he had convulsive fits from indigestion it seemed kindest to shoot him and bury him in the large meadow round which he had so often careered in his wild youth. Even at that great age his knees were smooth and unblemished, which was a proof of his mountain sure-footedness and the carefulness of his young riders and drivers.

Com was taught to do his task in the well-wheel by a man walking on either side, and soon, for about twenty minutes on every weekday, he stepped docilely on making the huge wheel revolve while one heavy oaken bucket went down and the other came up, brimming with ten or twelve gallons of perfect water. Meanwhile the elderley groom, one of the leaders at the Baptist Chapel at Poynings, sat quietly reading his Testament between wheel and well. When the pony felt the bucket at the top he stopped, the water was tipped into a cistern to run into the house, and he turned and plodded on the opposite way. Once, when excited, Com broke into a gallop which his guardian could not check, for of course he was loose in the wheel. Crash went the bucket against the massive axle, and down went both, heavy chain and all, to the bottom of the well 150 feet below! Then what a fishing took place! Every strong rope on the farm, and I think some borrowed ones, were joined and with iron grab-hooks the old foreman patiently fished until battered buckets and broken chain were brought to the surface. The farm had its own black-smith's and carpenter's shop close by, so repairs were soon done, and I think it never happened again.

But in the very hot summers the well would run dry and drinking water had to be laboriously fetched from the springs at the foot of the Downs, half a mile below. Good water was essential to a family whose father had signed the Pledge in the thirties as an example to his workmen, so he decided to have the well deepened. Strong ropes were added to the chain and most carefully were candles sent down and, to my father's relief, burnt clearly, showing there was no poison gas to endanger the expert well-diggers engaged to do the work. They dug down ten feet deeper, struck a fresh fissure of water in the solid chalk, and never again did the well run dry until it was replaced by an hydraulic ram which brought water from the spring at the foot of the Downs, beating automatically year after year without any attention.

After the main lesson of the well-wheel was learned, the pony was turned over to the elder children for a rather unconventional education. He had much handling and petting, but a little sterner discipline might have improved his manners, for he was never trustworthy with strangers. I have seen one of my brothers ride him into the dining room, and round the table, tolerated by my mother, who had been fond of riding in her youth in the thirties and forties. Her habit of heavy brown cloth, incredibly long and full in the skirt, like that in the contemporary pictures of Queen Victoria, was still extant, but I never saw her ride.

To us, living 'six miles from everywhere', when the Downs were innocent of wire fences, riding was our chief recreation. From our very door to Lewes Gaol was eleven miles of perfect primeval turf and we avoided roads, which were then regularly strewn with sharp flints, only slightly raked aside in the summer. The fees at the toll gates, too, were a consideration with such a troup. I remember one midsummer morning when two boys and three girls started at six o'clock to explore that remote wilderness called 'No Man's Land' at Shoreham — then so lonely, now so populous as 'Bungalow Town'.

We crossed the old narrow suspension bridge, our country horses shrinking from the gleaming water on either side, turned on to the beach, and rode to the only building there in those days, the now ruined fort at the harbour mouth. From this issued a number of soldiers, all in the scarlet coats of the period, who stared at us as if we had been a company of ghosts! The horses with larger hoofs got on best on the shingle, Com, the pony, being left behind, much to his disgust, for his ambitious little nose generally led the troup. Where a sward had grown over the pebbles he got on better, and a brother alighted and collected the strange sea plants we pointed out, tying them to my eldest sister's saddle (with the piece of strong string which always comes out of the pocket of a genuine country man) to be examined at leisure at home.

After the two boys next above me in age had been dispatched to their Yorkshire School the pony became more than ever my companion. We had but one delivery of letters daily about 10 a.m., brought from Beeding by a walking postman, but by some mysterious arrangement evening letters could be obtained at Hurstpierpoint four miles to the northward, and it was often decreed that pony and child would be suitably employed in fetching them. I think by that time toll gates had been abolished but to stick to roads did not satisfy me. I made up my mind to find a new way each time I was sent. Newtimber Hill, now given to the National Trust, and Wolstonbury Beacon furnished plenty of tracks and sheep paths to be explored. Arrived at Hurst I rode up on the pavement and tapped the Post Office window with my whip. The letters were brought out and buttoned securely in the breast of my little home-made habit, and I trotted off to find still another way home.

We had inherited from my grandfather a little low gig, built to his own design and perfectly unique. It answered well for our country purposes, being just the size for the Commodore. He could be lazy in harness, but let a black pig appear or loose horses in a field and he would fly along the road like a wild thing. I have thought it a piece of sublime un-selfconsciousness when my brother-in-law from a midland town drove that pony and gig along the parade at Brighton when it was used by scores of smart carriages and glossy pairs of horses, the heads and tails of the unhappy beasts being strapped together as tightly as possible to give what the coachmen of the sixties considered 'style', of which Com and his gig had none.

III. WINTER LIFE ON THE
SOUTH DOWNS

WHAT would modern young people think of the utterly quiet life on the Downs in winter, shut in by snow or rain, with no neighbours to associate with, no wireless, no gramophone, no piano (for we were a Quaker household) until later one appeared in the school-room simultaneously with a German governess? Yet we were perfectly content and happy and never thought of our life as dull. Our parents never craved for more amusement, and the quiet life was the usual thing for farmers in those days.

The only neighbours with whom we were at all intimate were a stately old couple of the all but extinct gentleman-farmer class who lived at Poynings Manor nearly a mile away. It was that kind old lady who gave me on my tenth birthday a root of lilies of the valley, which for nearly seventy springs has been my delight, its fragrant flowers blooming as freely in a little town garden as in the large one on the South Downs.

Only once do I remember an evening expedition in the sixties, on 10 March 1863, the day when the Prince of Wales, afterwards King Edward VII, was married to the fair Danish Princess Alexandra. That evening

my father packed the roomy 'chaise' with the good
governess and four or five of the elder children, and
taking a groom to soothe the nerves of a spirited and
unsophisticated horse, drove into Brighton to see the
fireworks and illuminations. These were much admired,
but I believe the strings of coloured lights were little
glass bowls, each containing an ordinary night light,
which had to be lit separately! How feeble they would
look by the fairyland of electric light in Brighton now!

The long winter evenings were always made cheerful
and happy by our parents. The substantial tea — the last
meal — was at six o'clock, and almost all the food was
home grown. A grist of wheat was sent to Ballard's
white windmill at Patcham and brought back as flour.
From this the large loaves were kneaded, and baked in
a perfect cavern of an oven in the old Tudor end of the
house, the large plain cakes in the same way, and we
had plenty of jam from the fruitful garden. The butter
also was home-made, but not the cheese which always
figured at tea time, sometimes Dutch cheese like a ma-
genta football, for which we children had a special
appreciation. The table cleared, two good oil lamps
were placed upon it, and we all sat round at our different
employments, father with his book and paper and with
his tired feet to the blazing wood fire, and mother with

FATHER & MOTHER

THE CELLAR STAIRS

THE BACK KITCHEN & SMOKE HOUSE

her overflowing workbasket, for eight active country children made abundance of sewing. She used to threaten to make me a leather frock! But at Christmas 1863 a London uncle presented her with that wonderful new invention, a sewing machine. It was a large, clumsy square thing in a walnut wood case—a 'Wheeler and Wilson' lock-stitch. It had a curved needle, most difficult to adjust, and was subject to irregular moods and tensions, yet it was an enormous help, for in those days every curtain, sheet and pillow case was made at home, as well as shirts and frocks. Few houses had a sewing machine then and it enabled my mother and sisters to send a larger contribution to the immense bale of clothing which the Brighton Quakers were sending to America after the emancipation of the slaves. Many hundreds of negroes, with all the mental helplessness which is one of the evil fruits of slavery, had drifted into a colder climate almost naked and simple warm garments were hastily fashioned and sent to the good friends working among them. My first recollection of needlework was laboriously hemming a child's frock of dull brown Winsey which my mother had enlivened with a little blue binding. We were glad to help with this, for the less tragic parts of 'Uncle Tom's Cabin' had been read to us and we always ate our meals from a set of picture plates given us by an old servant, with very crude illustrations of Eliza on the ice, Tom and Eva, and George Selby giving liberty to his slaves; so to be able to do our tiny bit towards the relief of those who had been slaves appealed to us.

Father would sometimes turn from the fire to give the boys help with their chess — a very favourite game which resulted in all four becoming excellent players in after life. We had draughts and dominoes and a home-made card game called 'Families' in which we demanded of each other 'Bun the Baker's wife', and 'Bone the Butcher's son', and thought it very amusing. Ordinary playing cards were never seen. We did not know such things existed! But my chief recollection of a winter evenings' toy was waste paper! We cut out figures and houses with doors and windows to open; we folded it into boats, and cocked hats, and elaborate though useless boxes. Waste envelopes were turned to draw pictures on the back, and as we grew older mother would show us how to make acrostics and simple rhyming games. Can it be believed there were no illustrated advertisements in the sixties? The shipping news was headed by a tiny ship, not larger than a postage stamp, and these we cut out as 'pictures'. Then 'Glenfield Starch' began to insert in magazines two advertisements, with pictures of Queen Victoria and Princess Alexandra. These were seized with joy, and daubed with all the colours of the rainbow from our little cedar boxes of stony cakes of paint.

There was always one break in the evening. We heard the door open and a step in the hall and one of the little ones would be told to 'Call Pelling in and set a chair for him'. Then the old foreman, whom father called 'One of Nature's gentlemen', would come in and take his seat modestly by the door to receive orders as to what each man on the farm was to do next day. He was a nice-looking old man, with thick grey curls and always a tidy linen round frock, embroidered on breast and shoulders by the skilful hands of his daughter. He was 'no scholard', although he had learned to read from his children, but he had the marvellous memory of those days and although master and man discussed a number of plans of work each man was in the right place next morning. Sometimes he would bring news from the outer world from which the heavy wooden shutters had closed us in. 'The foxes was just about barkin' up in the furze', he would say, and we rushed out to hear them. Once I remember his news was of 'northern lights', and from the carriage drive we saw the sky one glorious crimson glow of the Aurora Borealis.

Pelling could tell tales of hard times. He was probably a ploughboy at seven or eight years old. He had never missed a day's work in his life and had always borne the best of characters, yet when his children were young he had known what it was to start work with no better breakfast than a cold raw turnip! It was the knowledge of such sufferings of the many which made my father into one of the few corn-growers who dared to stand with Cobden and Bright in the 'hungry forties'. He voted at every election till past four score, yet never for a successful candidate! The daily paper he read was 'The Morning Star', afterwards merged in 'The Daily News'. The paper did not reach the South Downs every day, only when a team went into Brighton taking hay or straw and bringing back a load of stable manure to coax the barren, chalky 'layings' to produce a meagre crop of the then much desired wheat—those layings which have now 'tumbled down' into rough pastures.

After we started sending milk into Brighton the paper was brought back regularly.

Our evening amusements were always quiet ones, for father would read aloud bits of news which he thought would interest mother. I remember his sorrow at the death of Abraham Lincoln and his satisfaction when the savage prize-fight with bare fists became illegal and also when the law was made that executions should be carried out privately in gaols. It seems incredible that during my lifetime hundreds of English people would walk many miles to see a fellow man in his death agony, sent before his time to stand before the Judgement seat of God.

Apparently, however, the same morbid taste remains today, for if an especially gruesome crime has been perpetrated a portion of the public crowd the police courts; also, the fiction of gloves does not make professional boxing less degrading than the bare fist of the sixties!

I remember the day when education became compulsory — probably because an old family friend told me that now I must learn my lessons or the sister who taught me would send for the village policeman! The workmen's children walked daily a mile and a half to quite a decent little school which had been set up by the Squire's mother. The tiny parish was proud when a nice new schoolroom was built near the Church, but now it is empty and deserted, the educational authorities decreeing that it is too small to maintain. There was a charge of two pence per child each week. When three or four were of school age this was hard to find, and the teaching was valued accordingly. Needlework for the girls was made of great importance, to the great advantage of the homes of the future.

Our only party on winter evenings was having all the children of the workmen to tea. They arrived shy and solemn, their faces shining with much application of yellow soap, and their hair sleekly greased—probably with lard. We could not blame them, for in the sixties we all used 'pomatum', but ours came from the hair-dressers, scented, and in coloured glass pots. Tea in the kitchen wore off some of the shyness of our guests and then came games in the school room, such as 'Hunt the slipper' when a little impromptu conversation between cobbler and customer was received as exquisite wit. To finish there was a Christmas tree and what a simple and inexpensive joy it was! A home-made garment for each, pinafore, hood, or scarf, a bag of marbles, a penny Dutch doll gaily dressed, with a few bags of sweets, and col-oured candles.

One year we sought to make a variation by putting the gifts in the sack of a very mild version of Father Christmas, but it was not a success. The unsophisticated little natives who had never seen or heard of fancy dress took him for a bogey of the worst description and yelled with terror, in spite of the buxom cook's explain-ing 'It is only Master Louis inside!' So next year we went back to the Christmas tree which they knew and loved.

Quite early the fathers would come with yellow horn lanterns to guide the bairns to their cottage homes and we returned to the family fireside to laugh over the humours of the party. The winter evening ended with the children being dispatched to bed with flaring tallow candles in brass candlesticks, each with an extinguisher to suppress the objectionable smell when they were put out. The elder children remembered being sent to bed with a rush light. A long peeled rush which had been dipped in grease (the country people called them 'fried straws') was held in primitive iron pinchers, stuck in a block of wood, and it needed to be frequently pushed upward to keep it alight. A great bunch of rush lights still hung in the farmhouse attic in my childhood, and is now in Brighton Museum. White of Selborne praises them as the only means of light fit for the truly thrifty.

All windows were closed, for my mother, sensible and cultured woman as she was, firmly held the prejudice of her generation that 'night air' was unwholesome! Fortunately for us in the rambling house of twenty rooms not a window or door fitted closely, so fresh air was not wanting. Bitterly cold were the bedrooms, and hot bottles and down quilts were unknown, but we all had feather beds and plenty of blankets and took it as a matter of course to break the ice in the water jug in the morning. Those were not days of personal luxury for middle class folks. We were quite accustomed, too, to hear the rats take their nightly gallop in the hollow walls of the old house, knowing that they would not gnaw holes and come out, except occasionally in the kitchen regions. Once, alas, they penetrated to the playroom and nipped off the waxen nose of my beloved Arthur, a large bald-headed baby doll, who still exists, with his companion, Lily, who has a solid, shining china head and most pert expression, and who, although three generations have played with her, still squeaks cheerfully when pinched, in spite of her 68 years! Toys were not fragile in the sixties and having few we learned to handle them carefully.

THE TUDOR SCULLERY

THE BACK KITCHEN & FIREPLACE

BRIGHTON IN THE 1860s

IV. BRIGHTON IN THE SIXTIES

IT was no small advantage to live within six miles of so large a town as Brighton, but what a different Brighton it was in the sixties! The wildly gay days ot the Prince Regent were over and his costly, extravagant palace, the Pavilion, which with its many domes and pinnacles has been compared to an overgrown cruet stand, had been sold to the town by Queen Victoria. She came to Brighton a few times and my mother remembered seeing her stand on the steps of the White Hart at Reigate, a little upright figure in enormously spreading skirts of bright blue silk, with her tall husband beside her, while her six-weeks-old son was held up at the carriage window that the crowds might see their future sovereign. But the associations with her disreputable old uncles did not please the young Queen: the Pavilion was sold, and most useful its gorgeously decorated rooms have been for all sorts of local gatherings for some eighty years.

The Brighton that followed the Regency was a town of large lodging houses, resorted to by many invalids, whose Bath chairs were seen along the meagre parade and on the Chain pier, while others took their airings in the 'flys' which were the only public conveyances. It is comparatively recently that even a horse omnibus was seen in Brighton. Goat carriages were many, and donkeys for children's rides on the lower parade, but there was little scope for them on the scanty sands. We regularly drove into Brighton twice a week, over the Downs where our 'next door neighbour' was a small farm house three miles away called Tongdean. But there they kept a peacock and to see it in its glory was one of the excitements of the drive for the children. Where now trams run was a little narrow road between corn-fields. As we approached Brighton there was a black windmill and a little farther on a white one behind a house even then old, called 'Port Hall'. Over the front door was (and is) a figure of a knight in armour and on the side a strange bit of sham ruin with a gothic win-dow and a figure of a cowled monk in a niche. These figures gave us children our first impressions of sculpture.

We drove down North St., and into the Clarence Stables where for sixty years our horses were put up while the family, on Sundays and Thursdays, attended the Quaker Meeting for Worship in Ship St. It was the faith of our fathers for many generations. Our parents had each a many-times-great-grandfather who was a member of the Committee to enquire into his 'clearness of other marriage engagements' when that great man William Penn took as his second wife Hannah Callowhill of Bristol. His church membership was still with the small group of Friends at the little Meeting House now called by the strange name of 'The Blue Idol' at Thakeham.

So it was the natural thing for us to drive six miles to join in the quiet hour of worship, with no paid minister and no pre-arrangement whatever, in the Meeting House in Ship St. where there was always a lively and congenial gathering. Friends are invariably friendly and we children liked the warm greeting from many kindly folk. One old farmer's wife from the eastern Downs slipped into my hand every week for years a little parcel of barley sugar which sweetened our homeward drive. On Sundays we hurried home, as the governess and maids went to the afternoon service at the parish Church which was more than a mile away.

What appetites we had for Sunday dinner after facing the 'wild north easter', and often questioning Kingsley's taste in 'welcoming' it, as we drove home on the unsheltered road in the very teeth of it!

The butcher at Henfield, with whom we dealt for an unbroken seventy years, only came on Saturdays. The rest of the week we were dependent on game and home killed meat. So roast beef was the usual Sunday dinner, but before the joint was brought in we had a course of 'dripping pudding' — slices of light boiled pudding, some plain, some with currants, which had been under the roasting beef, and were, to our minds, perfectly delicious.

Sunday was a quiet, happy day. A long walk with 'Papa' in the afternoon, was followed by reading aloud, sometimes of the 'Pilgrim's Progress' while we sprawled on the floor arranging a beautiful set of cards, like Baxter prints, which we spread out to follow the adventures of Christian and Christiana. There was one good Sunday puzzle too, and I never hear the parable of the Prodigal Son without those gaily coloured scenes coming to my memory. After tea we read round some Bible story verse by verse, the little ones sitting by the parents and being helped to stumble through their verses. Psalms and hymns learnt in the week were then reverently recited, lessons which were never forgotten.

On Thursdays the Meeting for Worship was followed by a busy hour, the only time in the week that we saw a shop. Brighton drapers were small, one-man businesses in those days and the master of each would come forward to serve the quiet lady in the Quaker bonnet who had so large a family to buy for and knew exactly what she wanted.

Meanwhile our father, who was very particular that our growing feet should be shod with strong well-fitting boots (nobody wore shoes out of doors in the sixties), would take us to a shop where the master, a fiery little Radical, would pour out his opinions, listened to with rather amused courtesy by the customer while our boots were being fitted.

Shopping done, we drove home and after a hasty dinner father mounted his riding horse and returned to Brighton, with his pocket full of little bags of wheat and oats to attend the Corn market. This used to be held in a large room at an inn but father and some other sober attenders noted the disadvantage of being on licensed premises where some of the farmers would stay drinking until they were not very fit to drive home, even with horses which often found their own way as motor cars do not. So they petitioned the town for a public room and the large Riding School was let to them weekly, and is still called 'The Corn Exchange'. It was always needlessly large for the corn trade of a one-sided town like Brighton and gradually other business methods came in and the weekly market was needed no longer.

First of all the advantages of living near Brighton came — I think the word should be in large capitals — BOOKS!

To a man of my father's character the opportunity of obtaining plenty of good literature was an immense boon. He could not afford to buy many books, but a supply of the travels, biographies, and scientific works, which he loved, was a constant delight. Before he came to the neighbourhood in 1853, a group of Quakers, including good old Daniel Pryor Hack, who afterwards gave £600 to start the present Brighton Public Library, had fitted up a room at the Meeting House in Ship St. as a 'Proprietary Library' and had filled it with standard books. Each proprietor had a latch key, and books could be changed on Sundays. To us children, as well as to our parents, these books were a great satisfaction. There was little fiction, but 'Tom Brown's School Days' was there and Bewick's 'Birds' and the many volumes of Strickland's 'Lives of the Queens of England', Gordon Cumming's 'Hunting in South Africa' and Roger's 'Domestic Life in Palestine'. From there we got our first knowledge of Tennyson's earlier poems and laboriously copied out in manuscript books those that took our fancy — the homely country pictures of 'The May Queen', the magnificent musical rhythm of 'Blow bugle, blow', 'The Brook', and 'The Lady of Shalott'.

Catlin's 'Life among the Indians' and 'Hiawatha' enchanted us. We had two real buffalo robes brought by an uncle from America. We collected stiff feathers in the poultry yard and stuck them into soft stalks of rhubarb which, bound on our heads, bristled finely as we tried to reproduce the wild life of which we read in these favourite books.

My father did not read to us from the books in which he delighted, but anecdotes of the great men of the time, such as David Livingstone, were passed on to us. He not only read but remembered and could tell you to what height all the great mountains of the world soared — yet in his long life of eighty-four years he never saw a greater height than Ditchling Beacon on the South Downs! His knowledge of geography and natural history was amazing and always ready for use.

Farmers never dreamed of holidays in those days. The summer months, with haying and harvest, were their busiest times and with father's ambition to give all his eight children a sound education there was much of quiet self denial. Only once do I remember a brother persuading him to take his two eldest daughters to the Channel Islands. Yet he generally managed a few days at the great Quaker May Meetings in London — wishing he could have a saddle to sit on instead of hard forms! And then his treat was a few hours at the Royal Academy. The artists of those days, Landseer, Millais,

McWhirter, Faed, and Luke Fildes sent pictures which gave him profound pleasure. Frith never appealed to him, and for Sidney Cooper's crooked-necked cows and shaggy sheep he had a sublime contempt.

Quaker homes were simply furnished in those days and we had but one framed picture, a coloured print of the falls of Niagara. Father would say he knew what good pictures were and as he could not afford them he would not spoil his children's taste with the cheap and nasty. But he had in the fifties taken in a good 'Magazine of Art' and from its illustrations we got our first ideas of Raphael and Rubens, Greuze and Van der Veld, and the more modern Turner and Sir John Gilbert. He also had taken 'Chambers' Journal' from the very first when it was almost as large as a newspaper and in absurdly small print, yet we pored over those bound volumes and still more over the later ones with Mayne Reid's thrilling Indian tales. But as years went on the style of fiction changed and 'Chambers' admitted novels of such murderous and objectionable type that father decided that the 'Journal' should never enter his house again. But 'Good Words' never failed us. Edited by Queen Victoria's personal friend Norman MacLeod, each number was sure to have good reading, and the tales of Dinah Craik, George MacDonald and Mrs Oliphant were not of the sensational type. There were poems by Tennyson and Jean Ingelow, and the pictures were pleasing, and many a happy hour we spent making crude copies of them. The first visit to the town each month brought this favourite magazine, and also 'The Children's Friend' for the younger ones.

Our grandmother had given us a large book with many good woodcuts called 'Plates illustrative of Natural History'. To us it was 'The Animal Book', and on its second binding the simplified name was stamped. J. G. Wood's three-volume 'Natural History' of beasts, birds and reptiles was much loved and pored over during the long winter evenings.

V. AT SCHOOL AND PLAY

S C H O O L hours were scrupulously kept but, these over, we had the unrestricted run of the glorious Downs where in those days a stranger was seldom seen, unless when occasionally the now extinct Brighton Harriers swept by, with their livery of dark green coats. Hares are not an exciting quarry, as they are apt to run in a circle and the Southdown Foxhounds were more popular, their red coats making gay spots on the landscape. Curiously these coats are spoken of by the initiated as 'pink', though really of the brightest scarlet.

We children had very few restraints on our wanderings, but in winter the great chalk quarry, a favourite play-ground in summer, was strictly forbidden because the cliffs were apt to give way in frost. Enormous masses sometimes came down, bringing with them the jackdaw's nests of the previous season. This was a convenience to the lime-burners, who split them up to pack in the kilns below. Many waggons came from the low country to fetch the newly burnt lime — some for building purposes, some to spread as manure on the clay fields, both arable and pasture. Another warning was to beware of adders, which in the sixties were plentiful on

THE OLD FARMHOUSE: NORTH & SOUTH SIDES

THE SHEPHERD

the Downs. The country folk would have warned us against the really innocent slow-worm which is only a lizard with undeveloped legs. The work people called it the 'Death Adder', and I remember the cry of horror of a line of women raking hay when I picked up with an expression of pity a poor slow-worm which one of them had valiantly slain with her rake. It is much smaller than the true viper, which has a deep black zig-zag marking on the body — generally on a grey ground, but one once crossed my path with the background of a bright brick red, and a very handsome reptile it was.

My eldest brother was bitten as a small boy through putting his hand into a rabbit hole to see if a wheat-ear's nest with its pale blue eggs was there. Some weeks of discomfort with horrible nausea followed and one side of the child's body was black and blue as if he had been severely beaten. I have known half a dozen such cases but never a fatal one in Sussex.

The sheep were not infrequently bitten on the nose when grazing among the heather and would die, not from the poison of the adder but suffocated by the swelling. When the shepherd saw this beginning he would kill the sheep and cut off its head, as it could then be eaten as excellent mutton.

Eighty years ago my father set a price of sixpence on

every adder killed, and the workmen became very alert in looking for them so that they gradually decreased but are by no means extinct on the old farm even now.

When I was six or seven years old I found an adder curled up in the sunshine. I had sense enough not to attack it myself but fetched a sister twice my age, and with a mighty stick she slew the dangerous reptile and the reward supplied us with threepence each for pocket money. This was welcome, for it was one of my wise father's plans for his children that to teach us the value of money we had to earn it. Snails at a farthing a dozen from the garden were a chief source of income. If we wanted a penny very badly we hunted the clumps of day lilies and peered behind stones until we had forty-eight large, solid specimens of Helix aspersa — little ones did not count! These were counted out before one in authority and presented to the pigs, who received them as gladly as Whitstable folk do oysters on September 1 !

Our best source of income was locks of wool, for which we ranged the pastures where the flocks had been, picking off every morsel left upon a thorn. For this when the main crop was sold we got about a shilling a pound. Father's wish was to keep us out of doors and busy at some definite employment. We wanted badly a new saddle for the beloved pony, which would cost

three pounds, and we were told if we would earn half
he would pay the rest. Happily it was a great year for
haws and they were in demand to plant in a nursery
for future hedges. I forget the price, but we picked many
bushels and got our new saddle.

Outdoor amusements of all sorts were encouraged.
Of course we had a garden each, and a swing, and a see-
saw under the old yew tree which probably went back to
the time of the Knights Templars. When croquet came
into fashion father made us a set with the little stumpy
mallets of those days and eight different coloured balls.
A strip of meadow was added to the lawn on which
to set out the hoops. Later, when fashions changed, we
had a second set with long heavy mallets with stripes of
red and blue. The balls were made of yew wood. Some
large branches having had to be removed from the old
tree a few years previously, with the help of the old
estate carpenter these were turned on the lathe and
were quite as good as expensive bought ones.

The yew tree also provided our bows, but home-
made arrows are not easy to make with accuracy, and
we had a few shop-bought ones of which we had to
take great care.

When winter came we actually had home-made
skates — perhaps rough and clumsy looking but quite

good enough to provide many hours of happy exercise. Some others were inherited from a former generation — curious old Dutch skates, with a long hook in front. If these' became crossed in early struggles there were dire results! The pond was small, for water is scarce in Sussex, but it was large enough for a dozen skaters to disport themselves, though we rather grudged the square opening which was cut every day for the cattle. It was so shallow that when one moonlight night a friend and I crashed through in the middle we found our feet comfortably on the bottom, It was bitterly cold but we were close to home and dry raiment was soon donned.

The main London to Brighton road passed through one end of our parish and in the sixties was considered only for local use, although one four-in-hand coach ran in the summer to give Brighton visitors a taste of old times. Once only we saw a real post chaise, with a postilion in a light blue jacket and white breeches, riding one horse and leading the other, while a very old gentleman sat behind, evidently fearing to trust his person to the newfangled railway, although that had been running safely for twenty years.

In the sixties the toll gates were still in use. I think there were six in the depth of Sussex from Brighton to Crawley. Every few miles a white, locked barrier crossed

'THE SHEEP IS STILL DUMB BEFORE ITS SHEARERS'

GRANDMOTHER, THE CRAWLEY EDUCATIONIST

the highway and from the little two-roomed cottage would come hobbling forth an old man or woman to take the toll. The price was a shilling for four wheels, sixpence for two, and two pence for 'horse, mule, or ass', unattached to a vehicle. The calling of toll-keeper seemed to develop a certain crustiness of temper and malicious pleasure in keeping the traveller waiting, perhaps with an impatient plunging horse while, as slowly as possible, response was made to repeated calls of 'Ga-a-ate'. Change for coin was also a difficulty. How would the modern motorist like this cumbersome way of paying for the upkeep of the roads that he uses? In those days there were no steam rollers to smooth the highways. In winter a thick layer of flints was spread on the roads, to be gradually worked in by the iron shod wheels of the vehicles which passed over it. Every little parish repaired its own roads according to its lights. If the unpaid surveyor was conscientious and often used the road himself he would say to the road mender, 'No stone to be used which you cannot put into your mouth!', a test which we imagine was not often tried! If a farmer used a whole parish and kept no carriage he would sometimes take a spiteful delight in the badness of the roads which kept away the hated 'furriner'.

In the summer the loose flints were roughly raked to

the side but everyone who drove had to carry some tool to extract them from the horse's hoofs, and a messy business it was when the shaggy leg was soaked with mud and some sharp flint lay wedged between frog and iron shoe.

Was it in the sixties or later that the earliest bicycles appeared — first the 'bone-shaker', iron-tyred, wooden-spoked, with a nearly yard-wide handle bar? Next came the high steel bicycle with one tiny and one enormous wheel, only to be mounted by the most active young men, and a perfect terror to horses as they flew by.

One of our great treats was to be taken to see our grandmother at Crawley Manor House when father paid her his frequent visits. It was just eighteen miles, and a good horse with a light dogcart could do it in two hours and, after a long rest, return in the evening. What a contrast to the pace at which we rush about the country in these days!

There were interesting things on that main road for which we always looked out, such as an archway to a drive formed of the enormous jaw bones of a whale. This unique arch became smothered in ivy and has now disappeared. Where a stream crossed the road father would stop his horse that we might hear the 'beat, beat' of an hydraulic ram, which he admired as a useful new invention. The village of Crawley was dormant in those days. When the coaches were superseded by the railway and the industry of changing horses was over no one dreamed that it would revive again and become the busy place that it now is.

Grandmother was a good friend to that village. A farmer's wife and the mother of ten children, she was large-hearted enough to regret that the village children were growing up in complete ignorance. She started first an old-fashioned Dame School. Next she begged right and left among the local magnates until land was given and two schools were built, the second, called 'The British School' being so superior that a farmer, speaking of his early advantages, said that in those days Crawley was forty years before other Sussex villages in educational privileges.

An Infant school was a great novelty and a good little deformed woman reigned there for many years, much beloved by her small pupils. Boys wore frocks and pinafores to five or six years of age in those days, and as they filed out of school with a salute to mistress and her visitors the only way to distinguish sex was the pull at the forelock or the bob curtsey!

Grandmother also built a training home for girls, where many a neglected maiden got a good start in life.

The deeds of the house were so contrived that it was in the hands of trustees for 'the benefit of the neighbourhood' and it is now the Cottage Hospital, to which victims of motor accidents are carried, rather crowding out the country folk for whom the hospital was originally intended.

Directly school could be decently left country parents were eager to place both boys and girls in farmhouse service, where plain food was plentiful and the training of many a mistress of the Mrs Poyser type, sharp tongued but kind hearted, was 'the making of' a lad or lass whom she passed on to a higher class of service. A good woman died lately as a comfortably endowed widow who started in the service at nine years old, with the magnificent wage of 'sixpence a week, and her pattens and tuck aprons'. She was the eldest of a large family, all most thriftily brought up to earn their own living.

Looking at an old account book of the early sixties it is strange to realize what excellent and contented servants had incredibly low wages. One quite capable of simple farmhouse cooking, management of the dairy and butter-making, had only twelve pounds a year, paid quarterly, lest she should squander it, and untrained housemaids and nursemaids had six or eight pounds. But they not infrequently had gifts of a cotton frock which they were helped to make, and at Christmas pretty caps and aprons supplemented their meagre wages. No 'evenings out!' There was absolutely nowhere to go, but I remember quite cheerful, happy evenings in the kitchen with sewing, fancy work, and the books which were freely lent to them. In later years one of the farmer's daughters would spend two evenings a week in a very unconventional night school, ensuring that the knowledge picked up at the village school was not forgotten.

I remember my father asking a big lad who applied for the place of third shepherd if he could read. 'I used to be able to, Sir', was the reply.

At one time there was quite a good Evening School in an adjoining parish, taught by some young farmers, for the Rector had not the slightest interest in any of his parishioners although he took the stipend for half a century.

Some almost elderly workmen were eager to learn to read but they objected to using the children's primers of 'The cat sat on the mat' variety, so a number of large print Testaments were procured and the men could not feel as they stumbled through the sacred words that the task was beneath their dignity.

I have heard my father say that at the time of the

1861 census every single cottager asked him to fill up the papers, but by 1881 only one cottage had no inmate capable of doing it, and later it was done by all as a matter of course.

Gradually cottagers came to take the weekly local papers, and a bachelor actually had a daily which in pre-war days could be had for a halfpenny. But he gave it up at election time, 'for I don't know nothin' about 'lection stuff!'

VI. WILD NATURE ON THE SOUTH DOWNS

QUIET as was the South Down farm normally, we had occasionally a real sensation.

Once a large balloon came down in a meadow close to the house. It had started from the Crystal Palace but the aeronaut — one of the well known Spencer family — found himself drifting unpleasantly near the sea, so descended, catching his anchor in a hedgerow and tumbling from the car on soft hay. Of course all the few inhabitants rushed to see! The balloon looked enormous as we stood beside it and when the gas was being let out it rolled about like a huge animal. Mr Spencer presented my sister with a large bouquet from which some lovely pelagoniums were slipped, and bloomed in the schoolroom window — our only greenhouse — for many years.

Another less pleasant incident was when a cow which some butchers were driving to Brighton went mad and tossed a boy in the next village; happily he was not much hurt. The cow also tore up the potatoes in a cottage garden with her horns, and then came to a stand by a hedge on the edge of the Down, ready to charge at any one who came near. There were great

e

consultations among quite a group of followers, keeping discreetly in the background. Then we saw my
eldest brother with his rook rifle creep across the road
behind the poor creature, fortunately unseen. Sheltered
by the hedge he came near. As she turned towards
him a shot in the forehead rolled her over dead and a
great 'Hurrah' came from the group who were anxiously
watching.

We may be thankful that Government regulations
have saved England from the terrible danger of mad
dogs. A young farmer on an adjoining farm found a
stray dog worrying his sheep in their fold. Naturally he
went to drive it away and it turned and bit him, causing
his death from hydrophobia. Soon after, one of my
brother's beagles, a beautiful little animal, showed sus-
picious symptoms. She was shut up, but escaped and
rushed away up the Down. My brother seized his gun
and followed and shot the poor animal before any
mischief was done.

In the early sixties there was a shadow over Sussex
farms from which even children could not escape. This
was the Rinderpest, or cattle plague, a kind of bovine
typhoid from which valuable herds died off in a few
days. It was so prevalent that in an edition of 'Hymns
Ancient and Modern' which was published just then

there was a long hymn to be sung in Church 'In time of the cattle plague'! Our father was extremely anxious, for there was no compensation in those days, and to some farmers it meant ruin, but although it was raging within a few miles on either side of us it did not reach our valley.

The Foot and Mouth Disease, by which many Sussex farmers have lost cherished herds of pedigree cattle, was not in the sixties so much dreaded, and I have a vague remembrance of our teams of working oxen being nursed through it, and also some flocks of sheep, but they deteriorated sadly in value. At present there are very drastic regulations. If a herd is infected every animal must be slaughtered, and for a circle of fifteen miles no cow, sheep or pig must be moved without leave of local authorities. It breaks out so mysteriously that it is strongly suspected the infection may be brought by flocks of sea gulls or other birds from the Continent.

Of all the interests of the lonely farm no pursuit brought more pleasure than the love of natural history. Our parents both had the faculty of keen observation and to us young folk the ever changing life around made a fascinating study.

An old gnarled ash tree still stands on the Downs. More than 70 years ago three children perched in its branches—ten years old, eight, and six. One brought forward the proposition, 'We will all be great naturalists!' It was carried unanimously and although no greatness has been achieved, the ten-year-old became a great authority on Sussex birds and wrote charming articles in 'Blackwood' and other periodicals, the eight-year-old read papers at the British Association and published several books, the best known being 'Wild traits in Tame Animals', while the six-year-old has been able to pass on the interest in wild things, especially flowers, to quite a large circle. How well I remember my first Latin name! We had brought the Brooklime, with its blue flowers, from the stream at the foot of the Downs, and our mother, who had learned botany at her Quaker boarding school at Lewes, told us it had another name, 'Veronica beccabunga'. The word struck me as so exceedingly funny that I never forgot it.

The bird population of the Downs has certainly changed in the last half century. In the sixties the unmistakable croak of the raven was not infrequently heard, and Borrer says in his 'Birds of Sussex' that in 1855 they nested in a small plantation on Wolstonbury Beacon. Probably the reason for their disappearance is the decent law that all carcases of dead animals shall be buried. In the sixties the shepherds were accustomed, after removing the skin, to throw the dead sheep into any hole or copse, to the delight of the foxes and disgust of the violet-pickers.

This may account also for the disappearance of the grey, or saddleback crow, which used to be common in winter, but I never heard of its nesting on the Downs as the black crow frequently does — thief and cannibal as he is!

The quail were frequently heard in the standing corn, calling softly 'Bit by bit', or 'Wet my lips', as it is variously interpreted. They are late nesters, only arriving here in May, and the only nest I ever saw was accidentally stepped into by a reaper in harvest time. There were about fourteen eggs with glossy spotted shells, just ready to hatch. Every one was cracked, but with great care the contents were extracted, the poor little dead quails hooked out, and several decent specimens for the cabinet resulted. Only once did we know that the stone curlew nested in our neighbourhood. A workman rolling some young wheat saw an unknown bird with long legs and great yellow eyes like an owl, fly off before his team. Christopher did not serve a scientific master for nothing. He stopped his horses and found two large spotted eggs without an atom of nest lying beside a great flint. One egg was unfortunately stolen by the rooks, but we hope the other hatched out safely after we had inspected them.

Oh, those rooks! What a plague they were! It is small consolation to be assured that they are farmers' friends when they dig up freshly sown wheat, maize, and young potatoes, pull up the cabbage plants laboriously planted by hand for the cows' winter green food and, worst of all, strip the thatch from the wheat stacks in winter, spoiling far more than they eat by letting in the soaking rain. It takes a great many grubs and worms, which they really do eat, to pay for such mischief. Their natural enemies have been destroyed, and there is an overpopulation in the huge rookeries which are encouraged in the Weald.

The commonest bird of prey on the Downs is the kestrel, which is certainly the farmer's friend, destroying the swarms of field mice, especially the short tailed kind, or voles, which are very destructive to crops and even eat the peaches on the garden wall. No less than fourteen kestrels have been seen at once, poised in the air over a ridge where the little land lizards, called 'Effuts' by the country people, are plentiful and a favourite food of these hawks.

Among our country neighbours there were several colonies of badgers, accounted useful for their habits of digging out wasps' nests to eat the grubs, apparently quite careless of stings, but they also feed on the eggs of ground nesting birds and baby rabbits. They are so strictly nocturnal in their habits that they are seldom seen, but once in the twilight four young badgers in the playful puppy stage came romping close to my brother on horseback. They were used to animals in the pastures and did not perceive that this one had a rider.

In the autumn the badger gives vent in the darkness of night to the most weird blood-curdling screams as a call to his fellows. Foxes also have this Banshee-like habit, as well as the three-syllabled bark, 'Waff! Waff! Waff!' which is frequently heard. Foxes, although very trying to keepers of poultry, are really the farmer's friends. When an epidemic of mange cleared the foxes from our neighbourhood rats increased to a terrible extent, and rats are a worse enemy than many people realize.

Rabbits too increase so rapidly that they clear off the carefully sown crops like locusts. A startled mother fox in the early morning has been seen to drop from her capacious jaws eleven tiny rabbits which she was taking as tit-bits to her cubs. She was indeed a good neighbour on a farm.

It is wonderful that with so many prowling enemies the ground-building birds, pheasants, partridges and larks, manage to bring up their families in the grass of the Downs, yet of skylarks there is no lack and, except for a brief space in August when they are moulting, the air is full of their music even on winter days.

Town dwellers imagine that a lark can soar and sing indefinitely, but keep your eye on an individual bird and it is proved that three or four minutes is the utmost that the tiny throat and lungs can sustain the music, ere it sinks to earth to rest; but they are so numerous that there are always others to take up the strain.

In the sixties at the leading poulterers in Brighton there were dishes of small birds, nominally larks, trussed ready for roasting, and I believe for the true gourmand there were also wheatears, which shepherds were reported to catch in vast numbers. Curiously, since they were protected by law, wheatears have certainly decreased on the Downs, but of larks there is no lack, for they are reinforced by huge flocks from the tundras of northern lands.

It seems hard to speak against the 'blithe spirit' of Shelley, and the 'Bird of the Wilderness' of Hogg, but when these hordes arrive in the autumn and in thousands devour the first tender shoots of the newly sown wheat, the owner wonders if the taste for roast lark is so reprehensible after all!

Sentimental towns folk who feed the dear little sparrows in the winter have no idea that these birds spend their autumn holiday clearing off acres of ripening corn like a swarm of locusts. Farmers in the neighbourhood of towns are driven to grow the coarser, bearded wheat, as the long awns baffle the sparrows. When times were hard in the sixties, 'spar' pudden' was esteemed a treat in the cottages, the lads going round the stacks with a bat-fowling net, and catching them while at roost. One of the sparrow's worst sins is that when the housemartins, who are such good neighbours in clearing off the swarms of flies, have laboriously built their cup-shaped mud nests under the eaves the sparrow coolly drives them away, and takes the safe positions to rear his own brood at little cost of labour. The martin is a smaller and weaker bird, and can only submit. Once a cock sparrow who had done this deed was trapped by a long horsehair round the neck and his corpse dangled under the eaves all the summer as a warning to bird burglars.

The appearance of a rare bird was a great excitement at the quiet farm. Once we watched for a whole morning a hoopoe investigating the ant hills round the tennis lawn but never once did it rear its noble crest. An eagle, unmistakable by its digitated wings, once flew over — a rare sight in the south of England. We never heard that it was shot — the usual fate of uncommon birds — although a farmer might have some excuse if it were paying attention to his flocks of lambs.

A perfectly innocent visitor in the shape of a great white stork, which was flapping slowly over what to him must have appeared a dry and thirsty land, we watched one Sunday as we drove home from the Quaker Meeting. Three days afterwards it was shot at Rotting-dean and is probably in some museum.

Even the smooth hill turf was full of living interest.

We used to lie on our stomachs to watch the many small creatures which were pursuing their busy lives among the grass roots. There were grasshoppers, of course, and many ants, with their peculiarly business-like gait, bustling about in search of food for their community. A beautiful golden-green beetle about the size of a barley corn had a particular liking for the fragrant flowers of the mouse-ear hawkweed, and the scarlet black-spotted ladybirds were always a welcome sight to farmers, as in their larval state they live on the black aphides so fatal to beans.

Among the grass roots there was one beautiful creature whose species I have never found out. It had a little flat body of the brightest carmine tint, with legs to match, and crawled about rather slowly. It was like an enlarged specimen of that worst of summer plagues, the Harvester. In some districts this evil beast is unknown, but on the Downs it was common, and the poor little children whose parents were busy in the harvest field became a mass of irritating red blains. Gathering raspberries, plums or runner beans, always involved an attack of these pests.

The chalky soil provided shell material for multitudes of snails, many gaily striped and very pretty. One called the Elegant Cyclostome has a purple tip and the shape of a minute whelk. It is furnished with an operculum, or trap door, which has been known to catch by the leg a large humble bee as it crawled on the bank, so that it flew away with its captor. Among the moss in the copses was the glass bubble snail, with a perfectly transparent pale green shell, and many others.

Butterflies abound. Strong-winged Fritillaries rushing by, Chalk hill blues, often mistaken for harebells, as they perch on slender grass stalks, dainty 'Small Coppers' and Burnet moths, dark metallic green with scarlet spots. Every thistle flower or lavender scabious has its occupant.

Then there is the infinite variety of the Down flowers. How botanists from a distance revelled as we introduced them to the dark blue Roundheaded Rampion (Phytuma obiculare), the Star thistle (Centauria Calcitrapa), or the Field groundsel (Senecio arvensis). The dainty wee Moonwort fern (Botrychium Lunaria) could be found by those who searched for it humbly on their knees, and no less than twenty species of the orchid family grew near our own Downland farm. Bee, Fly and Butterfly, Frog and Man, with more or less resemblance to the namesakes, and many other beautiful kinds, including the tiny green musk orchis.

Probably I am the only person who ever picked a musk orchis on horseback; this happened as I rode in a deep lane with overhanging banks.

Quite unexpected vegetable neighbours sometimes appeared. The uncanny, purple veined flowers of the Henbane (Hyocyamus niger) suddenly sprang up near a barn. A single plant of the beautiful blue Salvia (Salvia pratensis) came on a rough chalky bank. It had never been seen in that neighbourhood before, but for more than thirty years it has bloomed there every summer.

My father had not been long at the farm before he found traces of a population which makes the Domesday book a thing of yesterday. The first find was a large smooth grey flint battle axe. This was followed by others carefully chipped which are really more ancient, and many household implements, such as scrapers, a flint saw, a quite workable gimlet, and hammer stones, one large one having been chosen by a right-handed man as the natural indentations gave a firm grip.

A pre-historic lady's china pantry was discovered when digging out a fox on the very summit of the Down with three different vessels which had lain hidden and unbroken for many centuries. The bronze age had left a quite mild little axe, spied on a newly turned furrow, and a dagger, lying by a female skeleton in a barrow which was opened when the British Association was held at Brighton in 1873.

A good many coins turned up in the course of years. A heavy Roman one which experts tells us represents the Roman Empress, Faustina Senior, the date A.D. 141, showed that the civilizing Roman influence reached to the Downs. A half-groat of Henry VII was pulled up with a mangold-wurzel and a large silver coin of Charles I was found under hill turf. A shilling of Philip and Mary and a slippery little gold five shilling piece of 1799 were later finds. The workmen, knowing that their masters were interested in such objects, became very acute in recognizing curiosities.

All these things added to the interest of the quiet country life and the taste for them was a great boon to the family.

A SOUTH DOWN FARM

The Head of a School in the west of England who was a keen naturalist said that he had *never* had a word of thanks from old pupils for the Latin, Greek and mathematics he had drilled into them, but from all over the world came letters from young men with grateful thanks to one who had opened their eyes to the wonders of the world around them.

VII. FROM FARM TO SCHOOL

FOR a couple with such educational ideals as those
which my parents possessed, the schooling of eight
children on the proceeds of a moderate sized farm was
a problem. Of course day schools were out of the question. For a single term, it is true, one little boy rode his
pony over the hills daily to Brighton Grammar School,
but this was not a success. It was a very cold winter,
and the long solitary ride in the early darkness could
not be hurried. It seems incredible that in those days
farmers deliberately preferred to drive without lamps
on their vehicles! 'It made young horses shy', they said,
and there was no law of the land to compel it. But not
once in the week would the schoolboy have encountered
a vehicle, in the three miles between his home and the
next door neighbour.

He heartily disliked the school. Excellent as it now
is, in the sixties things were slack, and there was a
French Master who one day, in lesson time, produced
a piebald beast dear to the schoolboy mind, and pro-
posed 'A raffle for a rat!' The next hour was spent
squandering the boys' pence for the master's benefit!

My family was deeply disgusted with this action, and
decided that the boy in question should have a different

type of education. In keeping with this, in 1866, my father took Ernest to Ackworth Schoool, near Pontefract in Yorkshire. This Quaker boarding school was founded in 1777 by Dr. John Fothergill, who, when looking for a suitable educational establishment for Quaker boys and girls, came upon a huge stone building erected for a Foundling Hospital. For some reason, this use of the building had been discontinued and he and others bought the estate for the Society of Friends. Many thousands of young people have had a sound education there, and the School still continues its useful career.

The journey to Ackworth was an immense undertaking for the little boy, who until then had hardly been out of sight of the South Downs. There is a legend that on the way northward father pointed out a strange animal. 'What is that?' The little farmer did not know — it was a white pig! In Sussex all the pigs of his experience were black.

Arrived at Ackworth, the boy soon said to his father, 'This is a jolly old hole!' and he was left happily at work and play for a whole year, for in those days the school had only a summer vacation. The difficulties of travel and the infections which some of the three hundred children would almost certainly bring back were reasons against frequent holidays.

There were bursaries and other help for parents who really could not afford the modest fees charged, but this my father's independent spirit could not accept, and he insisted on paying the full fee for his sons. When three of us were at boarding school at once, an unmarried brother and sister of my mother's nobly gave up their share of the rent of a modest house which had been left to the three, that the nephews and nieces might not lack a good education.

Ackworth life was on rather primitive lines in those days — stone or cement floors in the boys' dormitories and washing rooms, and the food very plain, if plentiful. There was a farm attached to the school, and two of the daily meals were large bowls of fresh milk, and slices of bread made on the premises by the old baker, Johnnie Walker, whose broad Yorkshire was an unknown tongue to the south country boys. When my brothers went on to a more advanced school, and had weak tea and bread and butter meals, they missed this good milk. Many years after he left Ackworth, Ernest, as a practical farmer, was welcomed on the School Committee for his help in the farm department.

Soon joined by his younger brother, he was very happy at Ackworth, and became one of the two most trustworthy boys who were chosen as Lodge Keepers,

with various responsibilities and privileges. He thorough-
ly enjoyed the games, especially cricket, and would
speak with profound admiration of the prowess of
Frederick Andrews, then an 'apprentice', as the young
teachers were called, who was afterwards for forty
years the much loved Head of the school.

After four years at Ackworth, the brothers went on
to Bootham School at York, where they wore 'top hats'
on Sundays. There was a good staff of trained teachers.
The science lessons particularly appealed to my brothers
and the school was endowed with a good telescope. In
many a night drive over the Downs Ernest loved to
point out the stars whose names he had learned at
York. The Minster and other old buildings interested
him. Being a good driver he enjoyed being trusted with
the pony carriage belonging to the Headmaster's wife,
but the flatness of the country round York oppressed
him, and I remember his keen delight in being once
more on his native hills.

After two years at York the boys returned home,
to enter the business world. Ernest was a born farmer,
and began at once to make himself useful on the home
farm. Louis was equally a born doctor, but it was some
years before way opened for him to take up the studies
he loved, and become in time a successful M. D.

The girls of the family did not need to go so far as Yorkshire for their education, as there was a good private school at Lewes. My mother herself as a motherless child had been very happy in a good school in that town, in the days when her weekly letter to her father at Reigate cost eightpence, paid by the recipient! Lewes was but twelve miles 'as the crow flies' from our farm home, and still among the South Downs which I loved.

'They must be assumed names—they are just like Dickens', wrote an old family friend to whom I had confided that I was soon to follow my sisters to the private boarding-school conducted by the Misses Rachel Special, and Mary and Catherine Trusted!

Never did parents specially entrust children to more utterly conscientious and kindly teachers than those three Quaker ladies, dressed in the primmest, neatest, plain gowns, and muslin or net caps, who always addressed their pupils as 'Thee' and 'Thou'. Their house, which is now the Lewes Post Office, is much larger than it looks from the street, but it was rather a tight fit for twenty-five boarders, and about half a dozen day scholars.

It was in August 1872 that I stood watching the carriage drive away in which my parents had brought the last of their eight children to start a boarding-school career. The parting was studiously cheerful and hopeful, and it never occurred to me to cry, but I felt rather forlorn, for I knew no one in the school, and was literally like a shorn lamb. I had been a 'Nazarite' till thirteen, and the day before the maternal shears had cropped the immense bush of flaxen hair which I could not manage to keep tidy by myself.

With me were left two heavy wooden boxes, probably made by the estate carpenter, with a neat outfit of clothes to last till Christmas, for we had 'halves', not three school terms, in those far away days. The smaller box contained books, a nice new workbox, and a real Winsor and Newton paint box, with moist colours, then a new invention, and good sable brushes. Years before a grandmother had given to each of us a golden sovereign which we were not allowed to spend, until mine bought the long coveted paint box, which I still use.

I soon made friends among my school fellows. Curiously, I was the only Sussex girl; the others came from Darlington, Birmingham, and quite a number from Essex, like myself the daughters of Quaker farmers. There were several charming Irish girls, who came 'to rub off their brogue'. A good deal of responsibility was given to the older girls, some of whom at sixteen had turned up their hair, and wore the fashionable but hideous 'chignon', a large round pad, over which the growing hair was spread more or less successfully. Our busy little German teacher, who was not well endowed by nature, showed little but pad!

Think of a girls' school without outside examinations and not a single piano! Only about a third of the pupils learned music, and all lessons and practices were arranged at the house of the Music Mistress nearby. We had a drilling master weekly, who in the large playroom, without any apparatus, put us through exercises suitable for growing girls. As we did not learn dancing, his wife came occasionally to teach us 'Deportment', making bows and curtsies, edging sideways between crowded seats, handing a book gracefully, and even walking up and down stairs.

We were near enough to Brighton to get good masters, and I remember with pleasure mildly scientific lectures on Light, Heat, and Electricity — but what an unfathomed power was the last mentioned sixty-five years ago!

We did not like the French Master, and accused him of giving good marks to the pretty girls, but the lessons of the Drawing Master were a weekly treat. Many of the girls chose large chalk heads which I thought rather useless, and with another girl I asked to learn to sketch from nature. Of course we began with many copies, but later were encouraged to portray the picturesque old houses on the other side of the street, and Lewes Castle Gateway, close at hand.

Our three mistresses were all most diligent. Miss Special, the cleverest and most feared, gave English Literature and German lessons. Miss Mary tried to make girlish fingers emulate her exquisite handwriting and needlework, and Miss Catherine's thorough teaching of Geography and Grammar — real old-fashioned Lindley Murray — were never forgotten. She taught me another lesson too. I had carelessly smashed a handsome vase in the school parlour, and expected a well-deserved scolding. When she saw my woebegone face the kind woman burst out laughing — 'That is the way to treat small misfortunes', she said, with never a word of reproof.

The school regime was rather Spartan. At seven a.m. summer and winter, we were expected to be in the schoolroom. Miss Catherine was always there before us, fixing needlework for the little pupils of the British School in which she took a great interest. We stood for a few minutes and repeated a Psalm together, or often the whole of Keble's morning hymn, for faithfulness in 'the trivial round, the common task' was what our mistresses especially desired.

An hour of strenuous 'prep' followed, and we were

quite ready for breakfast which consisted only of what we called 'doorsteps' — large slices of excellent bread and butter, and cups of weak tea. Twice on Sundays, and on Wednesday morning, we walked in procession through the town to the little Meeting House to join in the quiet hour of Quaker worship. To me, who found school life rather breathless, for at home my leisure had been spent wandering alone, or on my pony about the Downs, these quiet breaks in the week's duties were particularly welcome.

What would the modern girl say to the awful fact that we had no organised games? In the large playroom was a jumping-board, an excellent swing, on which we played some rather dangerous pranks, and on wet days or cold winter recesses jumping the long rope was cultivated to a fine art.

The daily long walk was our chief exercise, and Lewes was an excellent centre for a variety of walks — real country walks, with lovely wild flowers to collect, and and to name with the help of our mistresses.

So passed my happy school days. Why do people sneer at schoolgirl friendships? With three of those companions, now elderly women, I have kept up a vigorous correspondence all these sixty-five years, and their friendship was a lasting pleasure when I returned to live the utterly quiet life of my native valley. There I had many interests, bee-keeping being my especial hobby, both pleasant and profitable.

One by one the family drifted away until Ernest and I only were left. The farm was now owned by him, as our landlord had been about to sell it over our heads, and we loved it too well to allow that.

On the death of this brother in 1925, the land was bought by the Corporation of Brighton, because their excellent water supply is drawn from beneath it. The place is a good deal changed, but the hills remain, full of memories of happy farm life for sixty-six years.

So end the memories of the quiet Quaker home and of the farm life of my childhood. Although it has been sold away from the family and the land is well farmed by a stranger, I still love to visit my native valley. The ever spreading new houses of Brighton and Hove have not yet approached it within three miles, but the once grass-grown main road is travelled by innumerable motors. A telephone wire crosses the valley to the old house. Many of the arable fields have been roughly fenced with wire, and 'tumbled down' into pasture land again. Sheep are fewer and cows many, as milk-production is now the farmer's stand-by.